WALKING in DALBY

the great Yorkshire Forest

with other forests of the

North Riding Forest Park

by

J. Brian Beadle

First published in Great Britain in 2001 by Trailblazer Publishing (Scarborough)

ISBN   1 899004 37 8

© J.Brian Beadle 2001

Trailblazer Publishing (Scarborough)
Stoneways
South End
Burniston
Scarborough. YO13 0HP

MAPS

The maps in this book are not to scale and are for guidance only. They do not accurately portray the right of way. It is the readers responsibility not to stray from the right of way and it is strongly advised that you take the relevant Ordnance Survey map with you on the walk.

WARNING

Whilst every effort has been made for accuracy neither the publisher nor the author bear responsibility for the alteration, closure or portrayal of rights of way in this book. It is the readers responsibility not to invade private land or stray from the public right of way for walkers. All routes in the book should be treated with respect and all precautions taken before setting out. Any person using information in this book does so at their own risk.

ADVICE FROM FOREST ENTERPRISE

Members of the public are generally welcome to walk wherever they want on Forestry Commission land and to cycle or horse ride on many tracks, trails and roads. These forests are working forests and parts of them are closed from time to time to allow tree management to take place. For your own safety please obey any warning or prohibitive signs you may encounter on your walk and be alert for other users.

Surfaces of all tracks and trails vary according to the weather and time of year. Please ensure you are properly prepared and equipped for your walk.

Forest Enterprise
An agency of the Forestry Commission

CONTENTS

A SCENIC WALK TO THORNTON-LE-DALE

Thornton le Dale is one of the prettiest villages in North Yorkshire. It boasts a 600 year old village cross, a picturesque thatched cottage and well kept 17th century alms houses, all caressed by a babbling brook running through its main street. On route investigate the old church at Ellerburn which has connections with St.Hilda of Whitby. Watch the trout jumping at Paper Mill Farm and linger awhile to watch the wildlife in the Forest Park.

The Facts

Grading - Easy/Family
Distance - 8 miles (13km)
Time - 3 hours
Start/Parking -Low Dalby Visitor Centre, grid ref.857874
Map - Ordnance Survey Outdoor Leisure 27
Refreshment - Cafes and pubs in the village and Low Dalby
Public Toilets - Thornton le Dale and Low Dalby
Book Guide - Twelve Scenic Walks around Ryedale, Pickering & Helmsley by J.Brian Beadle has similar walks. Available from the Low Dalby Visitor Centre, Bookshops and Tourist Information Centres.

Your Route

Leave Low Dalby past the Visitor Centre towards the houses, keeping them on your left. The tarmac road soon becomes unmade and as you leave the houses behind you enter the forest. Pass signs for Little Dale, Flax Dale, Heck Dale and Sand Dale. Keep straight ahead at all times. Nearer to the water on the right there is a public hide for observing the wildlife. Continue through a couple of gates and through a sheep pasture to Paper Mill Farm. Once past the farm follow the public footpath sign to the left and where the track forks go right. At the top of the hill turn right onto the road then just before the main road turn right again along Church Lane for a quiet walk past the church to Thornton le Dale village.There are many facilities in Thornton le Dale. Cafes, toilets, pubs, shops and best of all, delicious home made ice cream at Baldersons!

When you have had a good look round the village head back the way you came as far as the bridge. Do not cross the bridge but turn left onto a footpath alongside the stream and past a pretty thatched cottage. Soon turn left onto a small road and when you reach the old mill yard cross the footbridge as directed and along the side of a large building. Soon cross a stile then continue on a footpath on the bank of the stream. Pass over a number of stiles on the river side path following the waymarks to a farm. Pass through the farmyard bearing left to exit along the farm drive onto the road near the church. Turn right here taking the road through Ellerburn, unless you have time to visit the interesting church. Soon the road bends to the right, ignore this and take the public footpath straight ahead. There are lots of fishponds on the way, watch for the fish leaping out of the water! The footpath continues through a field and eventually meets the forest at Ellers Wood. Take the forest road straight ahead which leads to the forest drive, bear right here onto the forest drive road down the hill to return to Low Dalby.

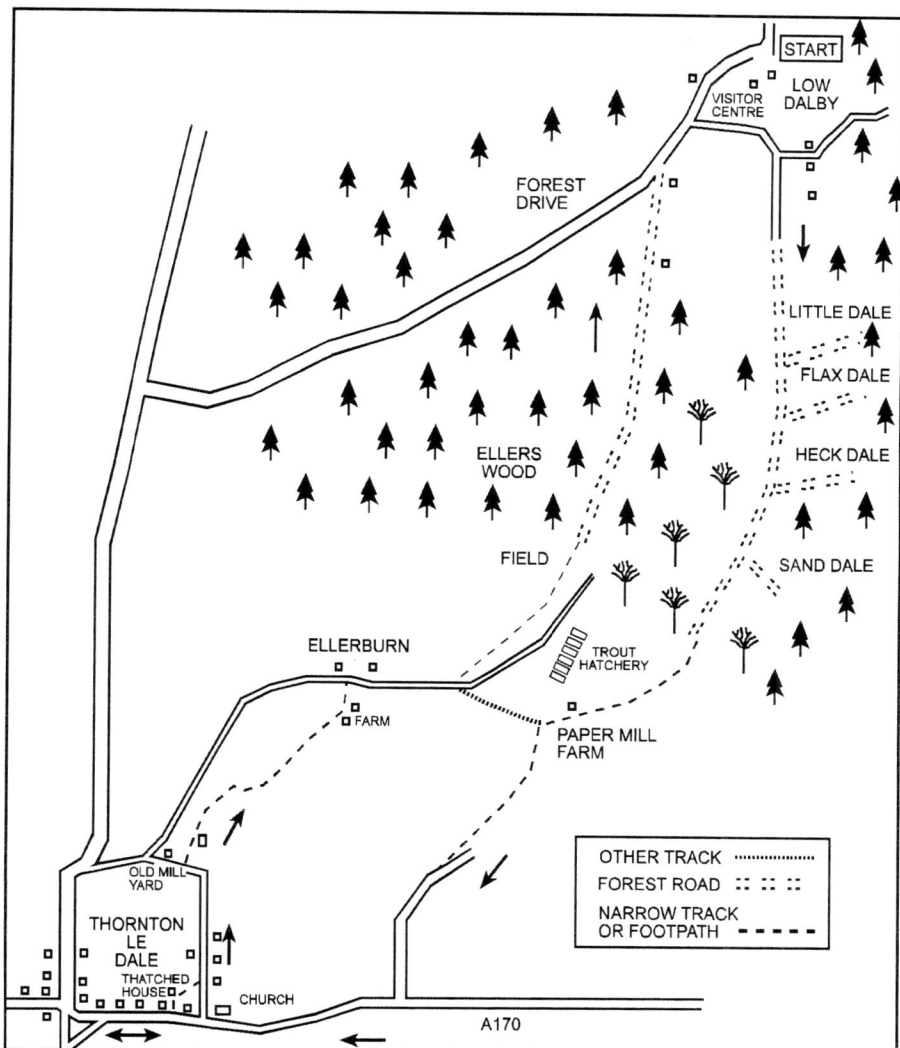

START

LOW DALBY

VISITOR CENTRE

FOREST DRIVE

LITTLE DALE

FLAX DALE

HECK DALE

ELLERS WOOD

SAND DALE

FIELD

ELLERBURN

TROUT HATCHERY

FARM

PAPER MILL FARM

OTHER TRACK ········

FOREST ROAD :: :: ::

NARROW TRACK OR FOOTPATH ▬ ▬ ▬

OLD MILL YARD

THORNTON LE DALE

THATCHED HOUSE

CHURCH

A170

OUTSTANDING VIEWS IN DALBY

Forest walks are not renowned for fantastic scenery, but this walk from the Bickley Forest Gate car park is the exception, offering two superb viewpoints overlooking Bickley, Langdale End and across to the North York Moors. The route is split into two allowing you to have two short walks or one medium length walk. The choice is yours.

The Facts

Grading - Easy/Family
Distance - 1½ + 3½miles (2.4 + 5.6km)
Time - Total for two walks, two hours
Start/Parking - Bickley Gate car park in
Dalby Forest, grid ref. 911911
Map - Ordnance Survey Outdoor Leisure 27
Refreshments - Low Dalby
Public Toilets - Low Dalby & Staindale
Book Guide - Walking around the North York Moors by
J.Brian Beadle has similar walks. Available from the Low
Dalby Visitor Centre, Bookshops and Tourist Information Centres.

Your Route 2

Starting from the car park walk towards the entrance then turn left onto a forest road guarded by a barrier. Continue along to a crossroad of tracks then turn left. In about one mile the track turns sharp left. Before taking this track look right and rest awhile on the seat to admire superb views towards Bickley. Continue along the forest track to soon arrive back at the car park.

Your Route 3

Walk to the exit of the car park, turn right onto the road then in a few yards go left into the forest. Soon a superb view appears on your right once again towards Bickley. Continue along until you meet a wide forest road. Go left here then at the 'T' junction turn right. After a pleasant walk you meet a junction of roads/tracks. Bear right here following the disabled sign then shortly keep left (do not go down the hill to the right) and soon reach the viewpoint at Crosscliffe.

Once again fantastic views present themselves. Let your eyes wander from the tarn on the right, then left past the farms of Bickley to the conical shape of Blakey Topping and past it to Newgate where a path known as 'The Old Wife's Way' takes you to Saltersgate, the North York Moors and towards the Hole of Horcum. This would be a good place to rest and take some refreshment before leaving by going left into the forest onto a narrow track which shortly crosses a road then re-enters the forest straight ahead to soon exit onto the forest road and picnic area. Go right now then follow the road left at the bend.

It is a long straight road now to meet the forest drive. Take care here and turn left onto the drive. As the road bends to the right, just after the Crosscliffe junction, look for a clearing on the right. Turn right here to enter the forest on a narrow track. Follow the main track as it bends left and right, past a seat to eventually meet the same crossroad of tracks you met shortly after the start. Turn left here then right at the end to return to the car park.

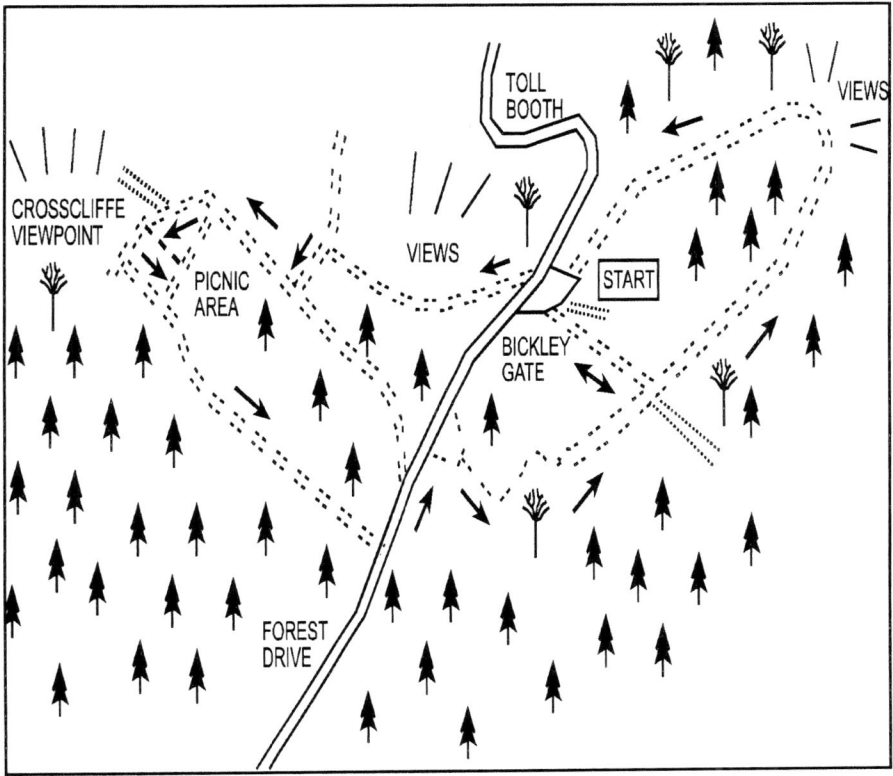

SUTHERBRUFF RIGG

Dalby Forest consists of amongst other things, lots of riggs and dales formed millions of years ago before man was 'invented'. This walk traverses one of these ancient riggs, Sutherbruff, which gives a welcome variation of scenery across to the moors when the tree line disappears for a short time. A pleasant walk which starts with a long but peaceful stroll gently climbing through Heckdale. The downhill section returns to Low Dalby on a multi-user track, so keep an eye out for cyclists.

The Facts

Grading - Easy/Family
Distance - 6 miles (9.6km)
Time - 2½ hours
Start/Parking - Low Dalby visitor Centre, grid ref.857874
Map - Ordnance Survey Outdoor Leisure 27
Refreshment - Small snack bar opposite the visitor Centre
Public Toilets - At the visitor Centre
Book Guide - Walking the Ridges & Riggs of North York Moors by J.Brian Beadle has similar walks. Available from the Low Dalby Visitor Centre, Bookshops and Tourist Information Centres

Your Route

Leave the car park at Low Dalby and head off in the direction of the Visitor Centre and snack bar. Continue along to a gate. Past the gate keep straight ahead with the houses of Low Dalby on your left then continue straight on without deviation. Pass signs for Littledale, then Flaxdale before reaching the junction of Heckdale. Turn left along the dale. This is a very sheltered dale with fairly steep sides. Not the most interesting or scenic of walks but very peaceful. It is about two and a half miles of gentle climb before you reach the 'T' junction with another forest road.

Go left here then shortly go left again along the dale signed as Flaxdale. Soon you come to a cross road of tracks. Turn right along the rough uphill track and continue straight ahead until you meet a wide forest road. Turn left now onto Sutherbruff Rigg.

There are good open views from the rigg, enjoy them while they last! Just past a large clearing turn right and when the road takes a severe left turn leave this road and keep straight ahead to join a narrow forest track going downhill. This is the multi-user track, beware! At the junction turn right to return to the Visitor Centre. Pop into the visitor Centre and have a browse you will find it interesting. When you leave the

Centre cross the road and have a 'cuppa' at the snack bar, then, suituably refreshed return to your transport.

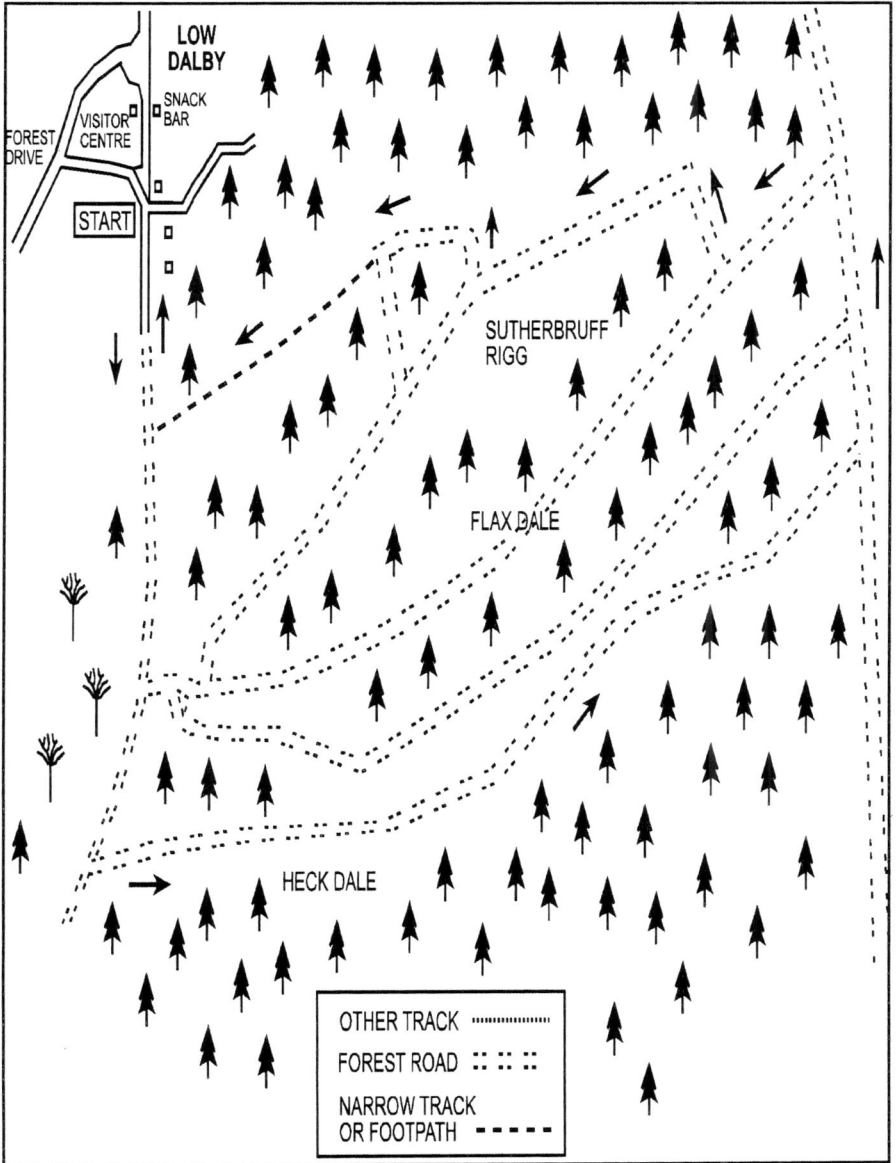

LOW DALBY

SNACK BAR

VISITOR CENTRE

FOREST DRIVE

START

SUTHERBRUFF RIGG

FLAX DALE

HECK DALE

OTHER TRACK ....
FOREST ROAD :: :: ::
NARROW TRACK OR FOOTPATH ----

SWAIRDALE & NEWCLOSE RIGG

Take a leisurely walk along Swairdale to visit the site of a long lost craft, rabbit harvesting! Approach the site from Dixon's Hollow and learn how the Warreners carried out their gruesome business. There is an excellent information board at the site giving details of the history of harvesting.

The return route is through an avenue of trees which eventually opens out across Newclose Rigg which has stimulating views into Swairdale before a devlish descent down the end of the rigg to return to the picnic area. The walk down the end of the rigg is rough and very steep, please take the utmost care if wet.

The Facts

Grading - Easy/Family if dry, Moderate if wet
Distance - 4miles (6.4km)
Time - 2 hours
Start/Parking - Swairdale Picnic area, grid ref. 860894
Map - Ordnance Survey Outdoor Leisure 27
Refreshment - Low Dalby
Public Toilets - Low Dalby
Book Guide - Walking around the North York Moors by
J.Brian Beadle has similar walks. Available from the Low
Dalby Visitor Centre, Bookshops and Tourist Information Centres.

Your Route

From the Swairdale picnic area walk along the forest road leading into the forest past the barrier. It is a gentle slope upwards for about one mile until you meet another forest road. Go left here then in a few yards turn right, still climbing. The road levels out soon with open views to the left. Ignore all other roads keeping straight ahead at all times until in just over half a mile the road sweeps to the right. Leave it here to go straight ahead into the forest on a grassy track. Soon the track falls steeply to meet a wide forest road. Turn left here to go downhill and soon look out for the rabbit warren on the right, where you can learn all about the harvesting of rabbits at the information board.

After visiting the warren continue downhill for about 170 paces. A grassy track goes both left and right here. Take the one on the left climbing up through the trees. Soon, at a junction of tracks turn right downhill into an avenue of trees. Continue along as the track sweeps round a long bend to the left then goes slightly uphill to meet a junction of tracks. Go right here then keep right again in a few yards. It is not long before you meet a wider forest road. Turn left onto the road and walk without deviation all the way along this road until it opens out into a clearing with good alround views to soon meet another forest road. Go straight across this road onto a wide grassy track. Shortly the track goes right at the edge of Swairdale. If you dare go near the edge you will see the dale far beneath you. Bear right now keeping parallel to Swairdale to eventually enter the forest. Follow this track until it sweeps sharply to the right. Leave the track here to go left down a very steep hill down the end of Newclose Rigg to return to the picnic area at Swairdale. Please take care if wet

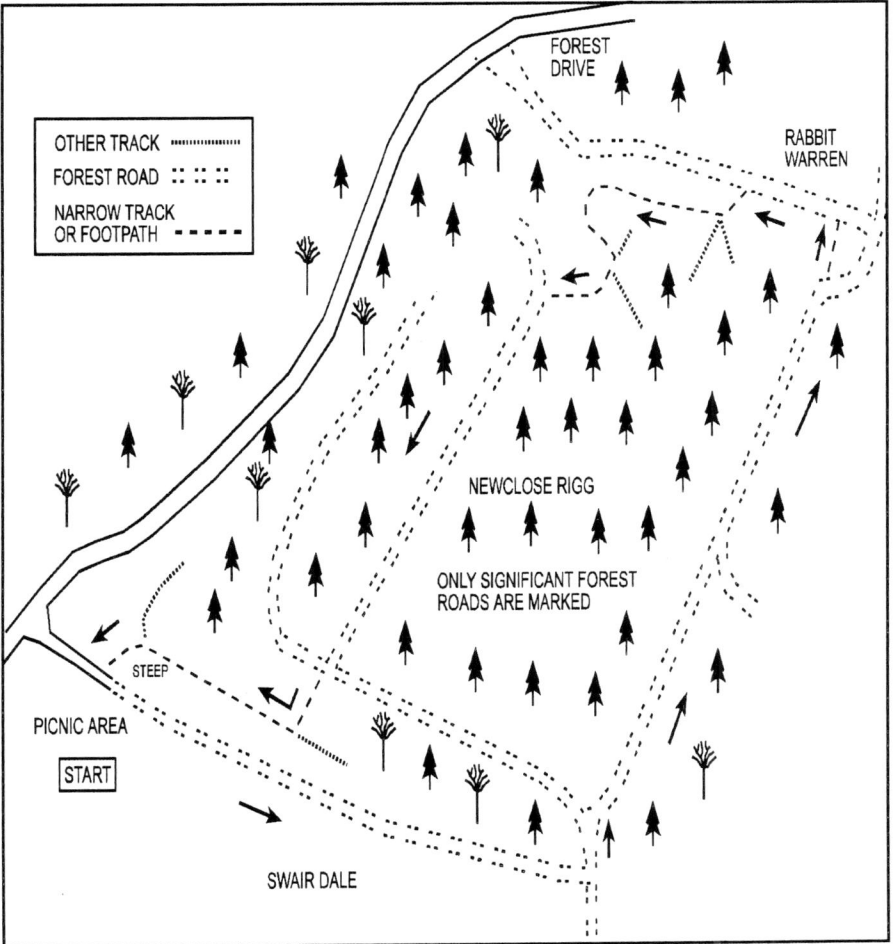

FOREST DRIVE

RABBIT WARREN

OTHER TRACK ··············
FOREST ROAD ∷ ∷ ∷
NARROW TRACK OR FOOTPATH ▪ ▪ ▪ ▪ ▪

NEWCLOSE RIGG

ONLY SIGNIFICANT FOREST ROADS ARE MARKED

STEEP

PICNIC AREA

START

SWAIR DALE

SNEVERDALE & DALBY BECK

Two short routes here which can be linked together to make one longer route. Dale, rigg and waterside walking are all in this superb route through Sneverdale and Sneverdale Rigg to cross the end of Seive Dale. Ice cream should be available along the way!

The Facts

Grading - Easy/Family
Distance - Route 6 - 3½ miles. Route 7 - 2 miles
                    Total 5½ miles (8.8km)
Time - 3 hours (Long route)
Start/Parking - Low Dalby, grid ref.857874
Map - Ordnance Survey Outdoor Leisure 27
Refreshments - Low Dalby
Public toilets - Low Dalby
Book Guide - Walking to Crosses on the North York Moors
by J.Brian Beadle has similar walks. Available from the Low
Dalby Visitor Centre, Bookshops and Tourist Information
Centres.

Your Route 6

Leave the visitor centre past the snack bar towards the houses. Pass the first houses then go left at the road. Shortly at the entrance to House Dale at the speed hump go left around the fir tree onto a narrow path into the forest. Keep on this path until it exits at the picnic area at the entrance to Sneverdale. Turn right into Sneverdale climbing gently into the forest. At the crossroad turn neither left nor right keeping straight ahead. In about one mile turn left at the 'T' junction. Soon you arrive at a junction of forest roads. Take the one downhill to the left. In a little over half a mile the forest road sweeps to the left. Leave the road here to bear right onto a grassy track into the forest. Downhill soon then when the track curves left take a track on the right downhill to the picnic area of Sneverdale. If you wish to finish the walk here you can return through the forest on the path you came on to the visitor centre.

Your Route 7

Leave the Sneverdale picnic area turning right onto the forest drive road. Just around the corner turn right into Seive Dale. At the rear of the parking area pass a barrier onto a forest road. Climb gently and when the field on the left ends leave the wide forest road to take a narrow path on the left climbing uphill through the trees. When you meet a wide grassy path go left onto it.

12

Continue along the grassy path enjoying good views until the wide path ends with the forest in front of you. Diligently look for a narrow path now diving steeply down into the forest on the left. Take care if wet it, becomes very steep and slippery. At the farm road turn left. Cross the forest drive road to enter a small gate at a yellow waymark into the grounds of Dalby House. (*There is a proposed right of way change here, please follow signs if implemented*).Keep strictly to the waymarked path around the house then left along the drive to eventually exit into a field. Turn left here along a sometimes muddy path. At the fork bear right onto the wider path which climbs into a field. Keep straight ahead on this path passing a waymark post along the way. Enter the forest at a stile/gate then follow this for half a mile almost to the road. Just before the road turn left at the waymark to take a short cut. Turn right then left at the road then left again to return to the visitor centre.

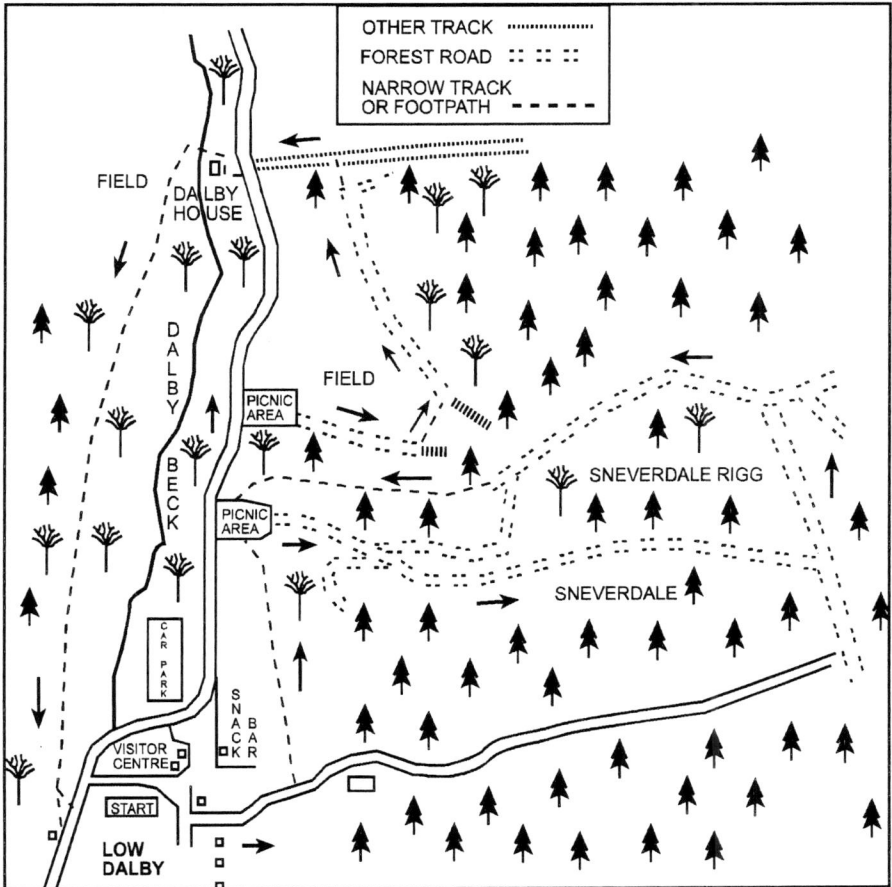

OTHER TRACK
FOREST ROAD
NARROW TRACK OR FOOTPATH

FIELD
DALBY HOUSE
DALBY BECK
FIELD
PICNIC AREA
PICNIC AREA
SNEVERDALE RIGG
SNEVERDALE
CAR PARK
SNACK BAR
VISITOR CENTRE
START
LOW DALBY

THE BRIDESTONES & STAINDALE LAKE

Enjoy this pleasant scenic walk to strange stones standing proud along the edge of Bridestone Griff and Dovedale Griff. The stones known as the Bridestones seemingly have nothing to do with brides being sacrificed or lovers throwing themselves off cliffs, which is a pity for I would have been to tell you a fine if gory tale. The word is probably from the Norse Brinkstones, or edgestones as the stones stand on the edge of a steep sided griff. The stones are interesting as they have weathered over thousands of years into strange almost Lunar shapes. On the return take a pleasant but short walk along the shore of Staindale Lake to take the opportunity to see the abundant wild life.

The Facts
Grading - Easy/Family
Distance - 6½ miles (10½km)
Time - 2½ hours
Start/Parking - Staindale, grid ref.878905
Map - Ordnance Survey Outdoor Leisure 27
Refreshments - Low Dalby
Public toilets - Near the parking area at the start
Book Guide - Walking around the North York Moors by
J.Brian Beadle has similar walks. Available from the Low
Dalby Visitor Centre, Bookshops and Tourist Information
Centres.

Your Route

You can start from the car park at either side of the road at Staindale or park where indicated on the road opposite the toilet block. If all these are full continue along past the lake to the hairpin bend and another car park on the right. Leave by the rear of the car park on the same side of the road as the toilet block. Continue along a path into the woods passing a bridestones sign along the way. Soon bear right to climb up into the forest. Where the path forks bear left and continue climbing, quite steeply, through the wood. At the top the path flattens and you get your first glimps of Low Bridestones. Soon join a stone paved path past the first stones passing many more on your way to High Bridestones across Bridestone Griff. The path descends into the Griff, crosses a small stream and ascends towards High Bridestones. If you intend visiting all the stones continue along, if not turn right onto a track near the first stone. At the fence turn left onto a wider track and follow this wide, straight track across the moor for almost one mile. Look out for two signposts. The one on the left with a small sign denoting National Trust, the other on the right with yellow arrows on it. Turn right here over a stile through scrub to soon meet up with a forest road. Turn right onto the road, glimpses of the superb Bickley scenery present themselves on the left. When you meet a wide forest road go right onto it. Then in a couple of hundred yards turn left onto an old, rough forest road. Keep straight ahead at all times to eventually meet a wide forest road, turn right here. At the next bend make sure you follow it round to the right to climb up a short hill. Eventually it descends towards Staindale. At the bend go left and continue downhill all the way to the Forest Drive road. At the road turn left then in a few yards follow the road round to the right and into the car park. Exit the car park on the path to Staindale Lake. Walk along the lake shore path which leads to the road side to return to the start.

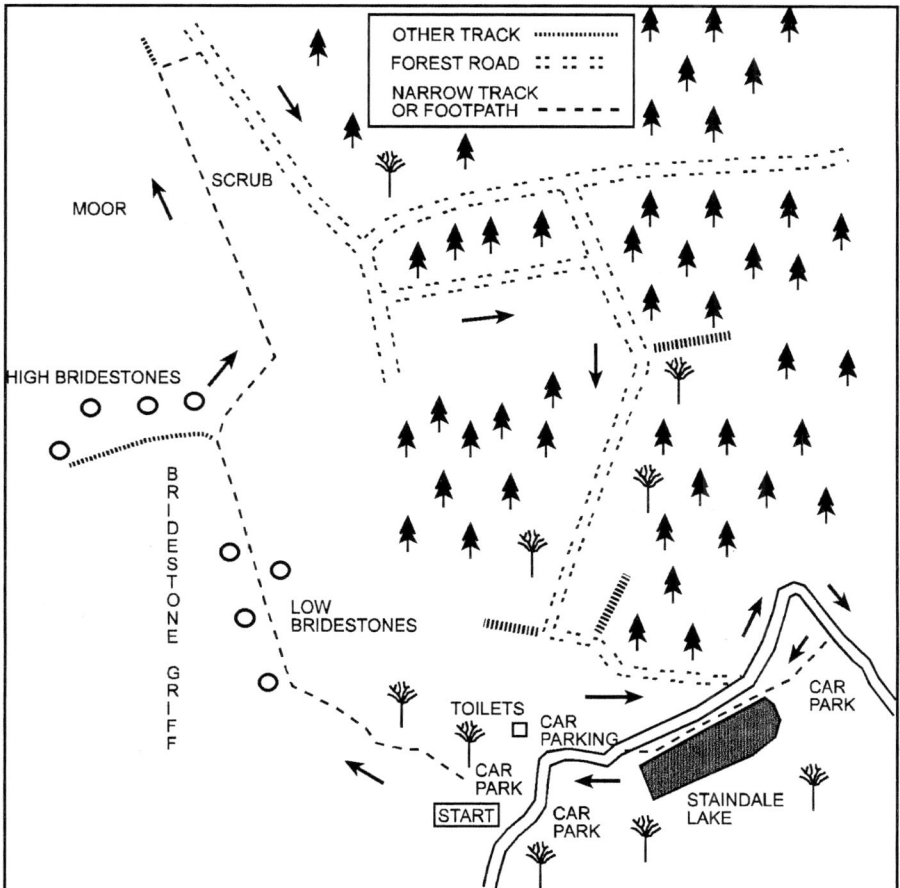

OTHER TRACK ·················
FOREST ROAD ∷ ∷ ∷
NARROW TRACK OR FOOTPATH - - - -

MOOR

SCRUB

HIGH BRIDESTONES

B R I D E S T O N E   G R I F F

LOW BRIDESTONES

TOILETS

CAR PARKING

CAR PARK

START

CAR PARK

CAR PARK

STAINDALE LAKE

CAR PARK

LITTLE SWITZERLAND

This walk into the hills of Bickley and Langdale End is full of surprises. It starts alongside the tranquil River Derwent which runs in the valley of the steep sided, wooded Lang Dale to where the river meets Harwood Dale Beck. Then climbs severely to the top of Barns Cliff into Broxa Forest. There are glimpses of magnificent views towards the moors and coast as you climb Barns Cliff end, with a seat for the weary at the half way point. The return through Broxa Forest offers breathtaking views over 'Little Switzerland', Langdale Rigg and the North York Moors. The hills and valleys around the village of Langdale End were given the name 'Little Switzerland' by the Victorians. I am sure you will agree they were right!

The Facts

Grading - Moderate
Distance - 6½ miles (10½km)
Time - 2½ hours
Start/Parking - Langdale End, grid ref 943910. Park on wide grass verge
Map - Ordnance Survey Outdoor Leisure 27
Refreshments - The Moorcock Inn at Langdale End. If you intend eating at the Inn it is advisable to ring to check if they will be open. (01723 882268)
Public toilets - There are no public toilets at the start. Only the Moorcock at the finish
Book Guide - Walking the Ridges & Riggs of North York Moors by J.Brian Beadle has similar walks. Available from the Low Dalby Visitor Centre, Bookshops and Tourist Information Centres

Your Route

Start from the bridge over the River Derwent at the bottom of the steep hill just after the Broxa junction. Cross the stile into a field near the bridge taking the public footpath through the trees along the river. Continue along an obvious path through woodland then open fields which soon becomes a forest track alongside the river. The path winds its way through the trees which vary from evergreen to deciduous. There is lots of wildlife in the woods, stop for a while by the river to look and listen, you might see a Kingfisher darting about. Eventually the path ends at a footbridge where the River Derwent is met by Harwood Dale Beck at a place known as Waters Meet. Do not cross the footbridge but turn sharp right and take the steep path up the end of Barns Cliff. Half way up there is a seat with good views across the North York Moors. Continue upwards and where the track forks keep to the right up the hill. Soon you arrive at a clearing, keep straight ahead here continuing upwards. The steep climb is almost over now as the track flattens out and eventually joins a forest road. Turn right here keeping straight ahead at all times through the forest. Where the forest road ends you have to turn left, but if you turn right for a few yards you will be able to admire the superb views across 'Little Switzerland'. When you can tear yourself away turn back and walk on a narrow path with the field on your right past the forest road you came on to another forest road. Turn right here and in about ½ mile pass through the village of Broxa. On leaving the village take the bridleway on the right at the corner at the top of the hill. Walk diagonally across the field to the road then turn right for a short walk back to your transport. If you would like refreshment, cross the bridge over the river and climb a short hill to reach Langdale End village and the Moorcock Inn.

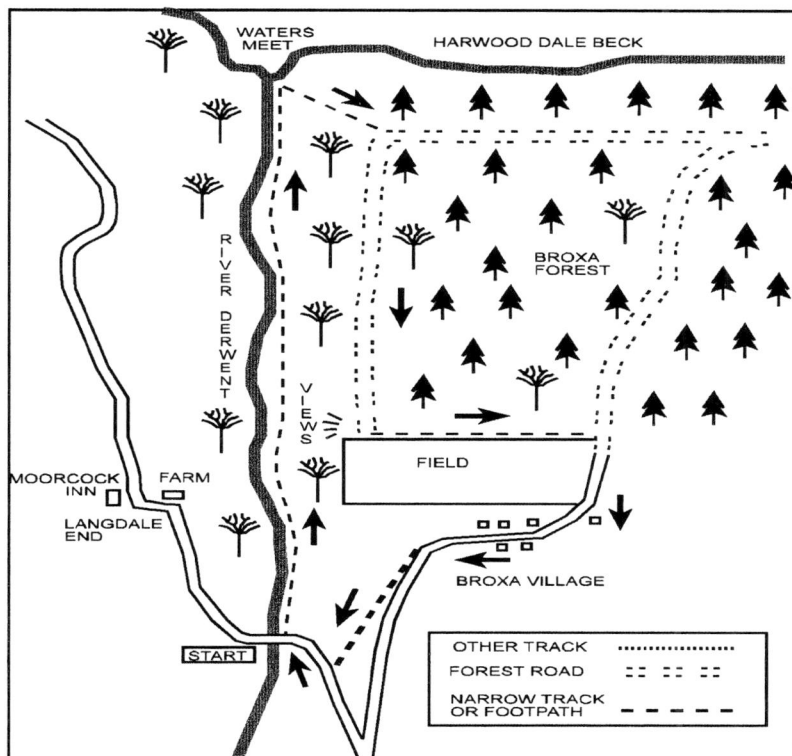

SCENIC STEAM IN NEWTONDALE

Take your camera with you on this superb scenic walk through Cropton Forest. You will find lots of interest as you walk through the forest which is home to Newtondale, although you will have to share it with the steam trains of the North Yorkshire Moors Railway. Enjoy the dale, the griffs, the forest and the steam trains, I did!

The Facts

Grading - Moderate
Distance - 8½ miles (13.6km)
Time - 4 hours
Start/Parking - Raper's Farm Picnic area and car park in Cropton Forest, grid ref. 824½939½
Map - Ordnance Survey Outdoor Leisure 27
Refreshments - The Horseshoe Inn, Levisham village

Your Route

Leave the car park turning left onto a forest road to descend towards the railway. When you eventually join another forest road go left. Half a mile from the start ignore the wide farm road on your right and keep walking until you reach see a bulrush pond on your left, a few yards past the pond go right along a wide grassy track to Newtondale Halt, this is a mile from the start. Cross the rickety stile alongside the large gate and pass under the bridge at the railway station. Turn left along a path between railway and beck. The path takes you over two stiles and a footbridge then climbs steeply into the forest. Soon cross the stile on the right out of the forest and continue to climb, very steeply at times and over a wooden staircase. At the top, turn right onto a path along the escarpment.The views across Newtondale to Skelton Tower and beyond are breathtaking! Soon the path goes left to join a wider track going right. Continue along this wide track passing Skelton Tower on your right. Continue straight ahead and to the road to Levisham Station. Go right now to descend to the station. Cross the track and enter the forest. Walk along the forest drive road for one mile until you reach a pair of holiday cottages, called 'Platelayers Cottages'. Just past the cottages turn left uphill on a forest road at the sign for Raindale. In a couple of hundred yards turn right uphill at the blue waymark. This is a narrow path and can be muddy for a short time if wet. Enter a field through a gate keeping straight ahead close to the fence on the right. Follow the fence left and uphill towards the house. When the fence turns to the right leave it and cross diagonally right uphill to a gap in the hedge in the top right hand corner of the field, then in a few yards through a small gate turning right onto the farm drive. Climb gently then through a gate into the forest. Keep straight ahead until you come to a crossroad of tracks at a severe left bend. Go right here onto a wide grassy forest track soon passing a blue waymark. Keep straight ahead on this track until it kinks right then left then soon leaves the forest . Turn right onto a wide forest road now. Walk for about half a mile until you pass through a double bend. Ignore the blue waymarks then in a couple of hundred yards look for a wide grassy track leaving the road at an angle. Take this path into the forest, cross a wider forest path to follow the waymark straight ahead on the grass track. Eventually the path narrows and descends to a very pretty steep sided griff, take care here! Cross a very small stream then climb on the obvious track to soon join the forest drive road. Turn right now down hill to return to the car park.

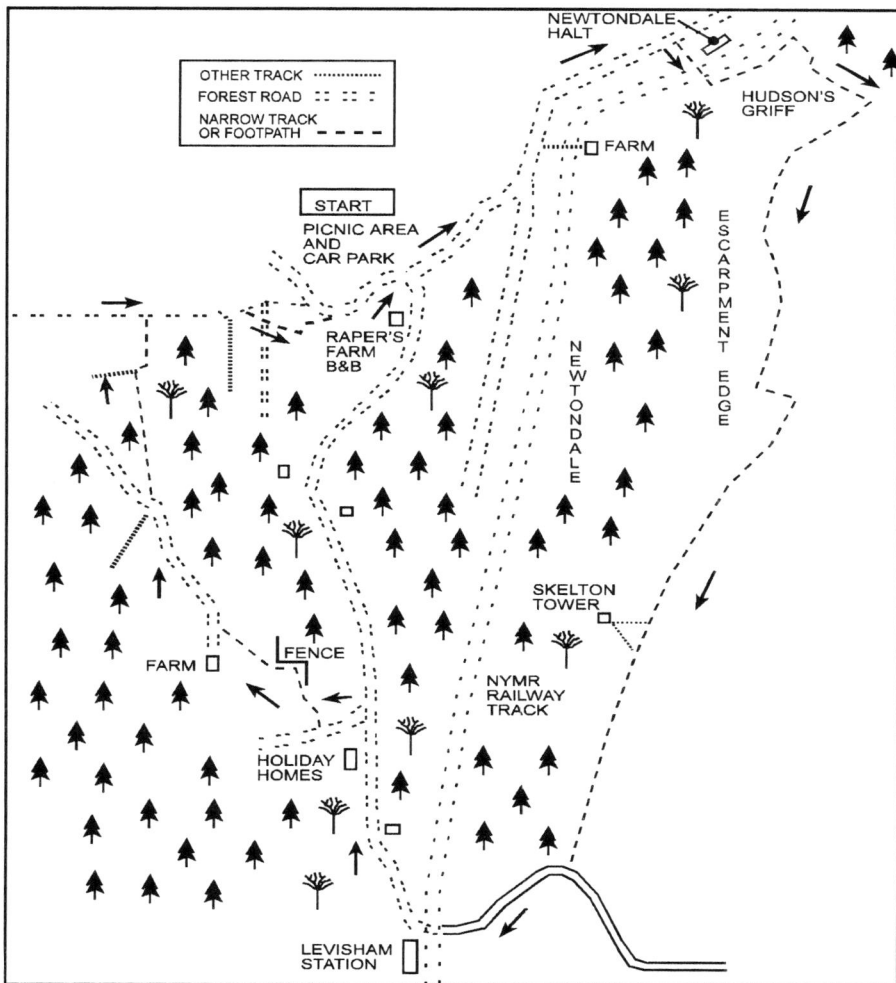

MAY BECK & JOHN BOND'S SHEEPHOUSE

Of all the forests in the North Riding Forest Park Sneaton must have the best features. A Hermitage, an old sheephouse, a high waterfall, a ghostly old house, gurgling becks, and a pleasant picnic area alongside a dark moorland stream all surrounded by beautiful heather moorland. There are two walks in Sneaton Forest which can be combined if you would prefer a longer walk of seven and a half miles. This is the first Sneaton walk the second is on page twenty two.

The Facts

Grading - Easy/Family
Distance - 3½ miles (5.6km)
Time - 1½ hours
Start/Parking - Maybeck Picnic area. grid ref. 892024
Map - Ordnance Survey Outdoor Leisure 27
Refreshment - May Beck, ice cream, crisps hot & cold drinks
Public Toilets - None
Book Guide - Walking to Crosses on the North York Moors by
J.Brian Beadle has similar walks. Available from the Low Dalby
Visitor Centre, Bookshops and Tourist Information Centres

Your Route.

Leave the car park and walk up the road you came on. In 100yds at a large stone turn right at the footpath sign. It is quite a pull up over a stile and through the bracken but the path is well worn. At the top of the climb exit over a stile into a field and walk straight ahead near to the stone wall on your left to pass by a ruined building to a stile. Bear slightly left over the stile to soon join a wide track bearing right and climbing to a gate at the top of the hill. Exit onto the moor and walk to a signpost at a crossroad of paths. Turn right onto a wide path which falls gently towards the forest. At the fork keep right then at the forest cross the stile bearing left onto a forest path. The path soon bends to the right and over a foot-bridge to John Bond's Sheephouse. This is a good place to eat your sandwiches! Opposite the sheephouse go left at the footpath sign and climb into the forest through a canopy of fir trees onto a golden carpet of needles. Keep almost straight ahead now on the most obvious path through the forest until eventually you meet a wide forest road.

Go left here then in a few yards go right then left onto a parallel forest path. Continue along to soon meet another forest road. Right now and downhill for a short way until you see a wide path on your right going into the forest with a confirming footpath sign. Walk downhill though the trees for some time, passing babbling becks until you meet a small gate. Continue through the gate then just before the footbridge at the bottom of the hill go right uphill through a small gate to climb quite steeply into the forest. As the path opens out watch out for a boggy section! Follow the obvious track as it becomes a narrow path again, twisting and turning as it climbs through the trees. At last the path descends to a footbridge. Go left over the bridge and follow the undulating path through the bracken which eventually descends to May Beck and the car park.

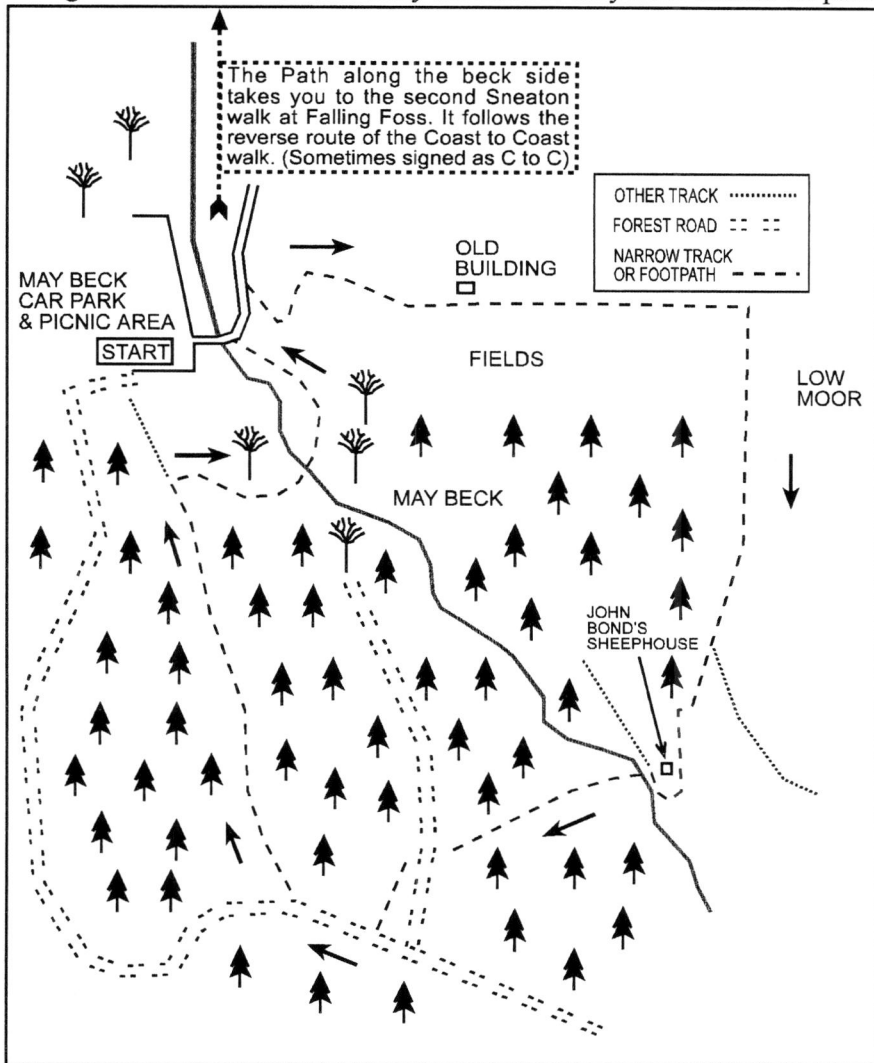

The Path along the beck side takes you to the second Sneaton walk at Falling Foss. It follows the reverse route of the Coast to Coast walk. (Sometimes signed as C to C)

OTHER TRACK ·············
FOREST ROAD :: ::
NARROW TRACK OR FOOTPATH – – – ·

OLD BUILDING

MAY BECK CAR PARK & PICNIC AREA

START

FIELDS

LOW MOOR

MAY BECK

JOHN BOND'S SHEEPHOUSE

LITTLEBECK & FALLING FOSS

There are two walks in Sneaton Forest which can be combined if you would prefer a longer walk of seven and a half miles. This is the second Sneaton walk, the first is on page twenty.

On this walk, probably the most featured of the forest walks, we visit a house hewn out of solid rock. It is called 'The Hermitage' though there was never any evidence of a Hermit living there. On top of the rock is a stone carved chair. Before the forest was fully grown the views from the chair would have been fantastic. Not far from the Hermitage is Falling Foss, a grand sight at any time, especially in winter when the frost freezes the spray turning it into an icy rain which clings to the rocks at the sides of the foss coating them with ice. Nearby Falling Foss is Midge Hall, a ghostly cottage in the woods, once the gamekeeper's cottage.

The Facts

Grading - Easy/Family

Distance - 4 miles (6.4km)

Time - 2 hours

Start/Parking - Falling Foss car park, grid ref. 889036

Map - Ordnance Survey Outdoor Leisure 27

Refreshment - None

Public Toilets - None

Book Guide - Short Walks around Yorkshire's Coast & Countryside by J.Brian Beadle has similar walks. Available from the Low Dalby Visitor Centre, Bookshops and Tourist Information Centres

Your Route

Leave the Falling Foss car park and walk uphill along the road you came on, pass a farm then continue climbing. If you hear panting and running behind you it might be the friendly farm dog. He will accompany you all the way on the walk! Opposite the house on the right turn left onto a wide track following the bridleway sign. At the crossroad of tracks near the farm buildings take the wide track bearing to the left. Cross the farm road then take the track almost straight ahead, do not follow the footpath sign!

Where the track forks bear right on an undulating path through the bracken to shortly arrive at Lousy Hill lane, further along you will realise why it is called 'Lousy Hill'! Turn left along the lane and head off down an ever increasing steep hill, enjoy the marvellous views as you descend. At the junction go left, soon to approach a very steep hill into Littlebeck. Where the road takes a severe right turn go left through a small gate at the sign for Falling Foss and C to C. The path enters the forest now and climbs, twists and turns for some time before reaching a cave. Climb the wooden steps over the top and continue through the forest until you climb to reach 'The Hermitage'. Leave by the right hand path downhill to the beck and a couple of footbridges. Cross the first one but ignore the second, instead follow the yellow waymark left uphill into the forest. The path climbs and falls bear right if in doubt. Eventually you see a sign. Exit here onto a stony road turning left to the stone bridge. To visit Falling Foss and Midge Hall go left here, to extend the walk to May Beck go right at the Footpath sign for the Coast to Coast. To return to the car park cross the bridge and climb the hill, the car park is on the right.

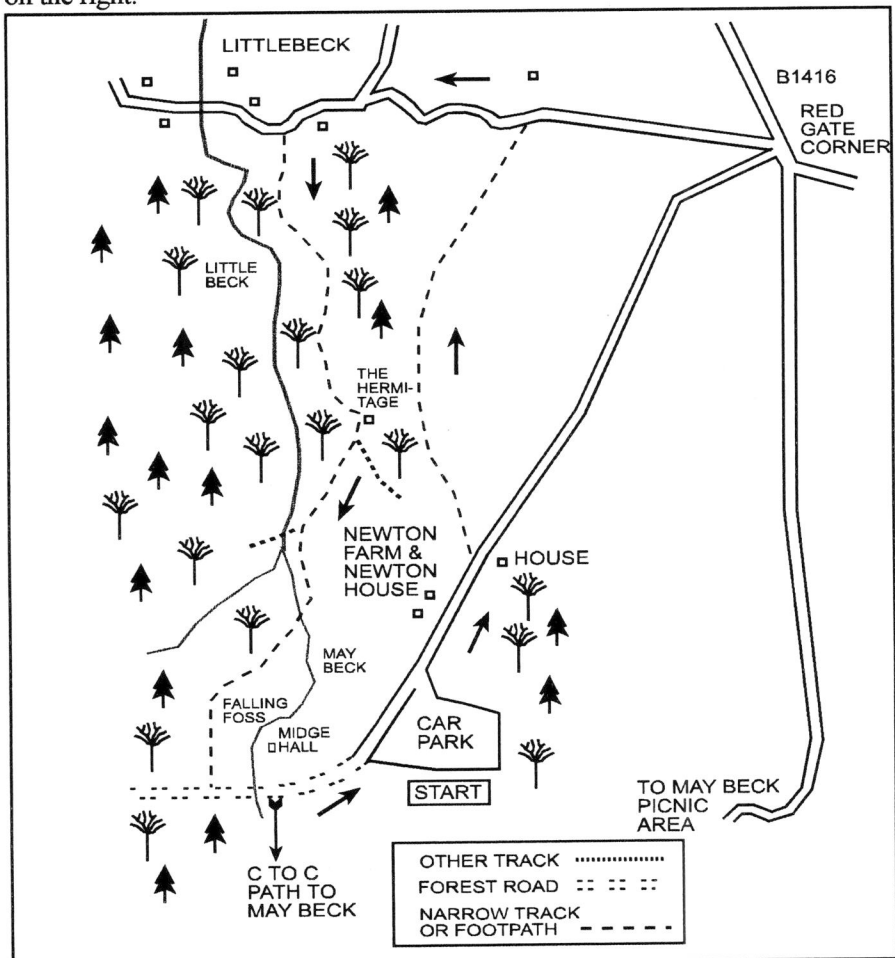

LITTLEBECK

B1416

RED GATE CORNER

LITTLE BECK

THE HERMI-TAGE

NEWTON FARM & NEWTON HOUSE

HOUSE

MAY BECK

FALLING FOSS

MIDGE HALL

CAR PARK

START

TO MAY BECK PICNIC AREA

C TO C PATH TO MAY BECK

OTHER TRACK ·············
FOREST ROAD :: :: ::
NARROW TRACK OR FOOTPATH – – – –

COASTAL VIEWS

Harwood Dale Forest is small compared to the vast acres of Dalby Forest. Nonetheless, it is capable of delivering a super walk with magnificent views to the south past Scarborough with its castle keeping a watchful eye from the headland to the sheer white cliffs of Flamborough Head.

The Facts

Grading - Moderate
Distance - 6 miles (19.6km)
Time - 2½ hours
Start/Parking - A171 at side of road on rough ground laybye near the Falcon Inn, grid ref. 969982
Map - Ordnance Survey Outdoor Leisure 27
Refreshments - The Falcon Inn near the start/finish
Public toilets - The Falcon Inn if taking refreshment
Book Guide - Walking around the North York Moors by J.Brian Beadle has similar walks. Available from the Low Dalby Visitor Centre, Bookshops and Tourist Information Centres.

Your Route

Starting from the rough laybye almost opposite the Falcon Inn on the A171 enter the forest onto a forest road at the barrier. Follow the road to the 'T' junction then turn left onto another forest road. The road soon dips then climbs around a severe hairpin bend. At the second bend at the top of the hill turn left onto a wide track into the forest which soon narrows. The track dips and climbs eventually giving good views across the ravine on your left. Towards the end of the track you could be attacked by foliage. Struggle through this for the last few yards to a forest road. Turn right onto the road away from the farm slowly climbing to a junction of tracks, go left here onto an open forest road with all round views. Continue straight ahead for some time then turn right at the end of the forest at the 'T' junction. In a little over half a mile go left at the crossroads along an old forest road. In a while it narrows and becomes more grassy turning right through the trees. It becomes narrowed but soon opens out again to join another road. Go right here then past the barrier and along the long straight which eventually curves to the right. At the crossroads (you might recognise them) go left, then before the double bends look out on your left for a path into the woods. This will lead you to a field and soon to the Harwood Dale road. Turn right then at the sharp left bend leave the road to go straight ahead through the gate. Follow the path round to the right then left until you meet a gate. Straight ahead here and soon into the forest again to continue to another gate ignoring the bridleway off to the left, this time into the open land. Walk around the edge of the field to the right opposite corner and exit through a small gate. Straight on through the grass, watch out for the bog!! At the forest road keep striaght ahead to the crossroads. Cross straight over and continue on the forest road climbing all the time. The road becomes narrow and eventually meets the forest road you started on. Bear left here to return to the parking area.

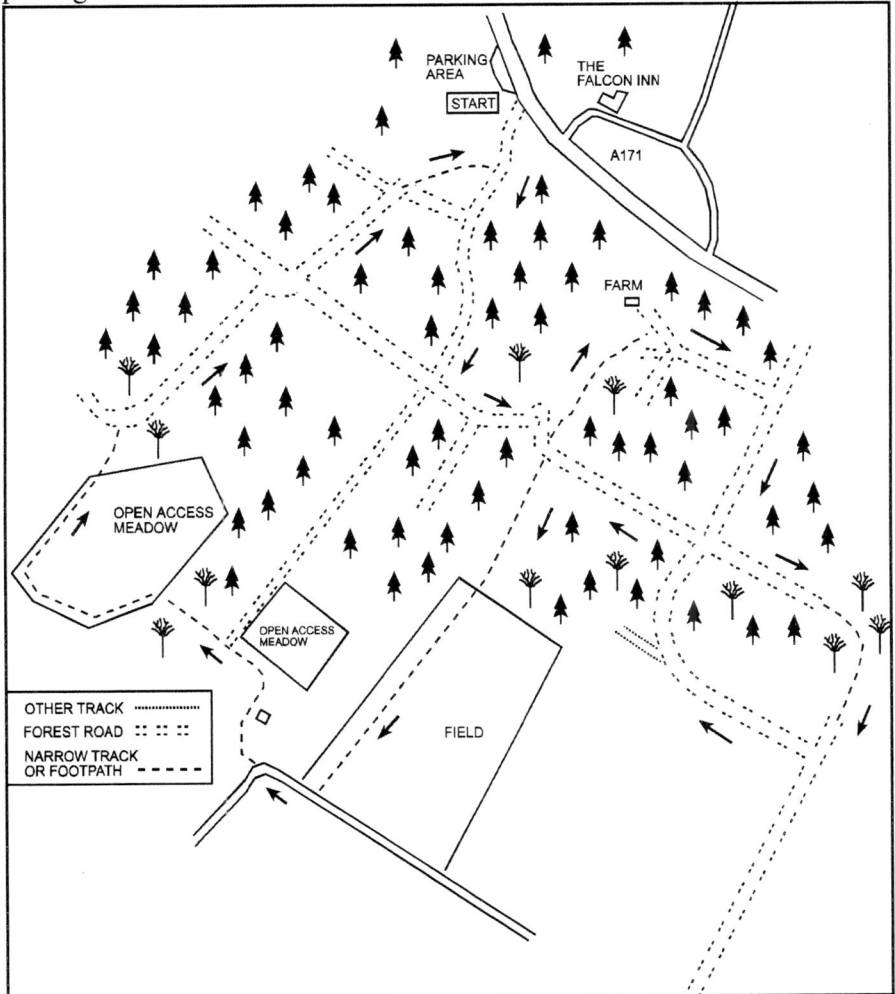

GRAND VIEWS ACROSS TROUTSDALE

The forest of Wykeham ends abruptly at Highwood Brow and Troutsdale Brow. They both overlook Troutsdale, surely one of the most scenic dales in the whole of Yorkshire. The grand views across the dale to the Derwent Valley and Langdale End are outstanding. The walk takes us through the forest to Troutsdale Mill, now a private house, then a steep climb along the road to re-enter the forest and return past the forestry nurseries and plantations along the escarpment, with another chance to view Troutsdale from a fine viewpoint.

The Facts

Grading - Moderate

Distance - 6 miles (9.6km)

Time - 2½ hours

Map - Ordnance Survey Outdoor Leisure 27

Start/Parking - Highwood Brow parking area, grid ref. 943889

Refreshments - None

Toilets - None

Book Guide - Ten Scenic Walks around Rosedale, Farndale & Hutton le hole by J.Brian Beadle has similar walks. Available from the Low Dalby Visitor Centre, Bookshops and Tourist Information Centres.

Your Route

Leave Highwood parking area and take the public footpath along the road down the very steep hill towards Troutsdale. Soak up the stimulating view across the dale but beware of the damaged road further down the hill. Continue along down the hill then turn left onto a wide forest road uphill into the forest. Follow this road for some way with glimpses of Troutsdale on the right. Note the farms, Troutsdale Hall and Troutsdale Lodge scattered around the dale and hills. When the road splits take the right fork downhll. Shortly, at the next fork keep to the main forest road to the left climbing slightly.

Keep on this main forest road to soon meet the Troutsdale road at Troutsdale Mill. Go left now uphill, follow the road round to the left at the hairpin bend and continue breathless to the top of the hill. The steepness of the hill gives you a good excuse to stop and soak up more grand views along the length of Troutsdale from this fine vantage point. At last the hill flattens out at the approach to the Cockmoor Hall parking area.

Turn left through the parking area to soon join a forest road leading to a gate into the forest at the 'link' signpost. Open fields on the right now and soon more forest then a plantation. Eventually you meet a tarmac road, turn left onto this road in the direction of the 'link' sign.

Pass Wykeham Nursery and more plantations as you head back to Highwood Brow car park. If you wish to have another tantalising glimpse of Troutsdale you can make a diversion left to the 'Raptor Viewpoint' where signed, then return to the forest road to continue your walk back to the car park.

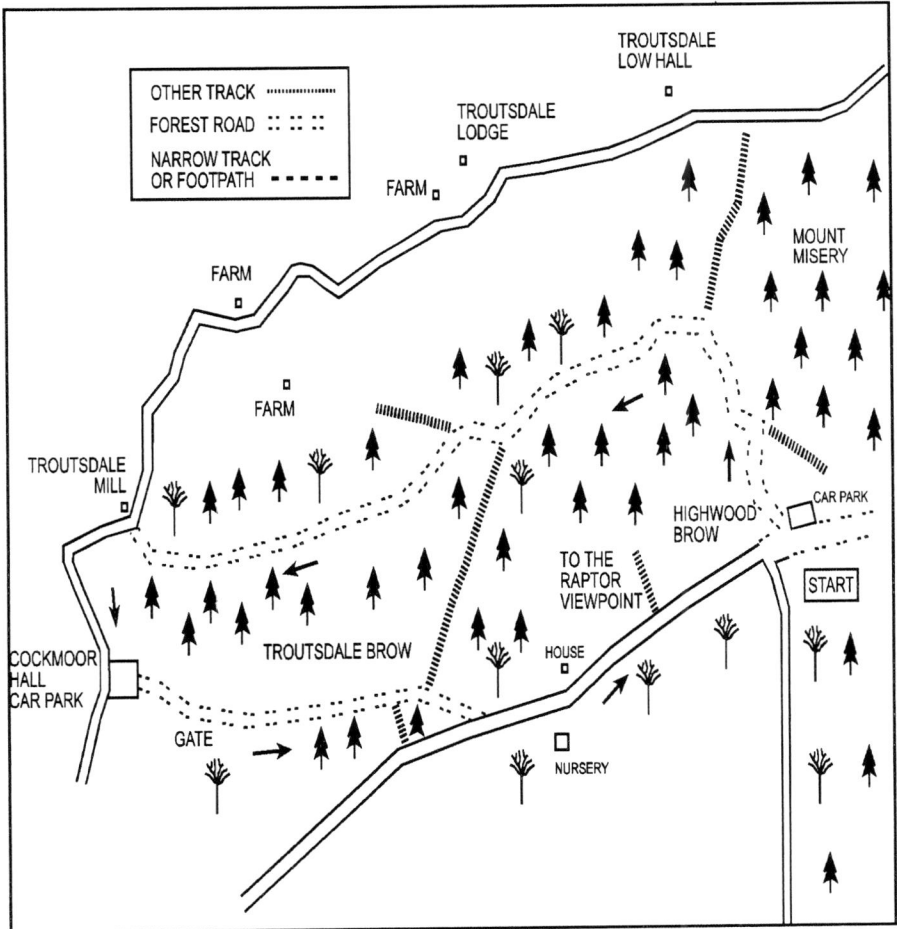

OTHER TRACK
FOREST ROAD
NARROW TRACK OR FOOTPATH

TROUTSDALE LOW HALL

TROUTSDALE LODGE

FARM

FARM

MOUNT MISERY

FARM

TROUTSDALE MILL

HIGHWOOD BROW

CAR PARK

START

TO THE RAPTOR VIEWPOINT

COCKMOOR HALL CAR PARK

TROUTSDALE BROW

HOUSE

GATE

NURSERY

OTHER TRAILBLAZER BOOKS

MOUNTAIN BIKING
Mountain Biking for Pleasure
Mountain Biking the Easy Way
Mountain Biking around North Yorkshire
Mountain Biking around the Yorkshire Dales
Mountain Biking around Ryedale, Wydale & North York Moors
Mountain Biking on the Yorkshire Wolds
Beadle's Bash - 100 mile challenge route for Mountain Bikers
Mountain Biking in the Lake District

WALKING
Short Walks around Yorkshire's Coast & Countryside
Walking on the North York Moors
Walking to Abbeys, Castles & Churches
Walks from the Harbour
Walking on the Yorkshire Coast
Walking the Ridges & Riggs of the North York Moors
Walking to Crosses on the North York Moors

THE SCENIC WALKS SERIES
Ten Scenic Walks around Rosedale, Farndale & Hutton le Hole
Twelve Scenic Walks around Ryedale, Pickering & Helmsley
Twelve Scenic Walks around the Yorkshire Dales
Twelve Scenic Walks from the North Yorkshire Moors Railway
Walking around Scarborough, Whitby & Filey

POCKET GUIDE BOOKS
The Crucial Guide to the Yorkshire Coast
The Crucial Guide to Ryedale and the North York Moors
The Crucial Guide to the City of York & District
The Crucial Guide to Crosses & Stones on the North York Moors

DOING IT YOURSELF SERIES
Make and Publish Your Own Books

OTHER BOOKS
Curious Goings on inYorkshire
The MG log Book
Triumph TR Log Book